Our world

Our clothes

from hat to shoes

Monica Hughes

Heinemann
LIBRARY

Little Nippers

www.heinemann.co.uk/library
Visit our website to find out more information about **Heinemann Library** books.

To order:
☎ Phone 44 (0) 1865 888066
▤ Send a fax to 44 (0) 1865 314091
▥ Visit the Heinemann Bookshop at www.heinemann.co.uk/library to browse our
catalogue and order online.

First published in Great Britain by Heinemann
Library, Halley Court, Jordan Hill, Oxford
OX2 8EJ, part of Harcourt Education.
Heinemann is a registered trademark of Harcourt
Education Ltd.

Editorial: Jilly Attwood and Claire Throp
Design: Jo Hinton-Malivoire and bigtop,
Bicester, UK
Models made by: Jo Brooker
Picture Research: Catherine Bevan
Production: Lorraine Warner

Originated by Dot Gradations
Printed and bound in China by South China
Printing Company

ISBN 0 431 16254 9 (hardback)
06 05 04 03 02
10 9 8 7 6 5 4 3 2 1

ISBN 0 431 16259 X (paperback)
06 05 04 03 02
10 9 8 7 6 5 4 3 2 1

British Library Cataloguing in Publication Data
Hughes, Monica
Our Clothes
391
A full catalogue record for this book is available
from the British Library.

Acknowledgements
The publishers would like to thank the following
for permission to reproduce photographs:
Angela Hampton p. **17**; Bubbles p. **9** (Frans
Rombout), p. **20** (Geoff du Feu); Corbis p. **8**;
Photodisc p. **10–11**; Sally and Richard Greenhill
p. **6–7**; Tudor Photography pp. **4–5**, **14**, **15**, **16**,
18, **19**, **21**, **22–23**.

Cover photograph reproduced with permission of
Tudor Photography.

The publishers would like to thank Annie Davy
for her assistance in the preparation of this book.

Every effort has been made to contact copyright
holders of any material reproduced in this book.
Any omissions will be rectified in subsequent
printings if notice is given to the publishers.

Contents

Choosing clothes

What will you wear today?

What's the weather like?

5

A sunny day

It's nice and warm so you don't have to wear many clothes.

Remember to wear a hat to shade you from the hot sun.

Warm clothes keep us
snug when it's cold.

A wet day

It's raining!
It's pouring!

Put on your raincoat and your Wellington boots to splash in puddles.

Splish!

Splash!

A snowy day

You need lots of
warm thick clothes
to play in the snow.

Have you ever made a snowman?

Sport

shorts

t-shirt

trainers

What do you wear when you go swimming?

15

Keeping clean and safe

A painting overall will keep your clothes clean.

Do you wear a helmet when you go out on your bike?

Careful!

Dressing up

Do you like to dress up?

You can be a prince or a princess.

Special days

Where do you think they are going?

Bedtime

Time for bed!

Index

The end

Notes for adults

This series supports the child's knowledge and understanding of their world, in particular their personal, social and emotional development area. The following Early Learning Goals are relevant to the series:
• respond to significant experiences, showing a range of feelings when appropriate
• have a developing awareness of their own needs, views and feelings and be sensitive to the needs and feelings of others
• have a developing respect for their own cultures and beliefs and those of other people
• dress and undress independently and manage their own personal hygiene.

Each book explores a range of different experiences, many of which will be familiar to the child. There is plenty of opportunity for the child to compare and contrast their own experiences with those of the children depicted in the book. This can be encouraged by asking open-ended questions like: How do you decide what to wear? Why do you wear different clothes when you go to bed?

The series will help the child extend their vocabulary. Some words related to **Our Clothes** could include *fine, light, heavy, waterproof, transparent, padded, plain* and *decorated.*

The following additional information about clothes may be of interest:
The material used for different items may determine their use – woollen gloves to keep hands warm, rubber gloves to keep hands clean. The weight of clothes can vary – a quilted anorak may be light and warmer than a heavy wool duffel coat. Clothes can sometimes indicate a person's job or role – a uniformed police officer or a lollipop man/woman.

Follow-up activities
The child could collect pictures of people wearing different kinds of clothes and suggest why they are being worn. They could make collections of similar items of clothing and compare and contrast them.